gone
sane

poems by
Christal Rice Cooper

Some of these poems have appeared in *Conversations At The Wartime Café: a Decade of War 2001-2011.*

Cover artwork by: Sue Messerly and Renée Sheridan
All artwork copyrighted by Christal Rice Cooper
Cover design and typesetting by Donna Biffar

Printed in the United States of America

ISBN: 978-0-9650764-4-9

River King Press
PO Box 122 Freeburg, Illinois 62243

For Wayne, Nicholas, and Caleb

I cherish my treasures.

Contents

The Lambs

the

celebrity

Jim Carrey, by Sue Messerly

Carrey Mad

for Jim Carrey

I said I was a rich movie star,
showed them the check
I'd written to myself
for $10 million.
For services rendered.

Everybody who knew me knew
I quit school
because my father lost his job
and I had to work
scraping pubic hairs from gas station urinals

where I made enough for us to eat
and buy gas for our house,
an old car,
faded and colorless.

Sometimes I drove
to Mulholland Drive,
parked on the shoulder,
walked to the edge and stared into the lights

until I believed
I was Hollywood's top star.

When I got the big break,
my father died.
I dropped the $10 million check into his casket
and watched it float to his chest.

Later that year I earned $10 million
for wearing a green mask
and carrying a rose in my mouth.

Maria Callas, by Sue Messerly

Sacred

All of them mystified by my voice —
thus the religion of Maria began.
Each one a believer.

But not that ugly, rich Greek.
Within a month we were lovers
onboard the Christina.

No longer the adored singing diva of the Greek,
but a willing worshiper
of a man who showed off his large
bar stools made from the foreskins of whales.

There were jewelry, furs —
but never his praise — especially
for my voice.

I stopped singing,
took long afternoon naps.

When I awoke he was always gone.
Before I could cry
I watched I Love Lucy —
so I could laugh.

When he married another
I watched it again.
But I couldn't laugh.

When he died I died too.
Now I am ash.
But not my voice,
echoing in a conch shell,
lying still in our marriage bed
of the Aegean Sea.

Joe DiMaggio and Marilyn Monroe, by Renée Sheridan

A Fiction Of The Rose

for Joe DiMaggio and Marilyn Monroe

I gave her the first rose
when she told how
she never knew her father
but dreamed Clark was her daddy.

And then – two roses of every color
when she said she loved
the Sisters' reading *Noah's Ark*.

She died with the phone
to her ear, listening
to a dead tone. Then,
a dozen red roses on her casket.

And one rose each year
for her grave.

When the doctor said
I'd be dead in six months,
I started searching
for the perfect rose –
the garden red rose
Babe Ruth had blessed
by the Pope
then gave to his mother.

Babe's grandson accepted $1,000.
And the rose quivered in my palm.
Delicate. On the verge of shattering.

It waits on my nightstand
next to my favorite picture of her,
and I remember how we read

The Hunchback of Notre Dame,
in bed, after making love.
She cried when Quasimodo lay
against the dead Esmeralda.

Now I dress in my best suit,
stretch my long body on the bed,
the rose on my chest.
I want to be ready when I wake up –
when hers will be
the first face I see.

My whole life has been decided by fate. I think something more powerful than we are decides our fates for us. I know one thing – I've never planned anything that ever happened to me.

– Sharon Tate
July 1969

Roman Polanski and Sharon Tate, by Renée Sheridan

Joshua Tree

The Joshua Tree was named by Mormon settlers who crossed the Mojave Desert in the mid-19th century. The tree's unique shape reminded them of the Biblical story of Joshua, who reached his hands up in prayer.

She liked being nude
while making love
or taking a bath.

If she'd had a chance in the Garden of Eden
she wouldn't bite the fruit.
She would be obedient.

Her mother wanted her to be a star.
And she was.
Miss Tiny Tot of Dallas.

Already then her skin was
creamy vanilla,
mixed with the dust of Adam's rib –

her hair,
a golden piece of sky
in the setting sun.

When she learned of the child
she knew
she would have the baby.

Her mother and sisters said
it would be
a girl – because her parents had girls.

Three of them. A trinity.
Her husband wanted a girl.
White lace gown, fragile hands,

teeth like snow
from the Swiss Alps
where they vacationed in winter.

Voice, a mixture
of Katie Holmes, Marilyn,
and Jackie O. Like a bird.

She hardly thought of Joshua Tree,
but somehow a baby
made the journey more potent.

Some things, **she said,**
are so beautiful
that you can't smile.

Growing up she spoke the rosary.
She quit without thinking.
Her mother liked to think

she at least thought about it.
And now that body
is slashed, a hole in her womb,

where no baby breathes.
Paul Richard wrapped now
in a cloudy shroud

within the dead arms
of his mother.
Her first words,

baby Paul's first words.
Her last words, his,
begging for his life –

Oh, Mommy. Oh, Mother.
Mother and son
reaching hands to the sky

in prayer.

Katherine Hepburn, by Sue Messerly

Steel Eggs

I told Miss Barbara Walters I think of myself as a tree.
She asked, "What tree would you be?"
Oak, I said,
breathing in the green air of life.

I have not lived as a woman.
As a child I wanted to be called Jimmy.
As a woman I am Mister,
dreading uncomfortable dresses,
preferring the tailored suits of men.

My habit of dress shocked
Mother's Catholic friends.
When they learned of my divorce,
I laughed as the eggshells crunched.

With Howard
the press called me
diamonds fizzing in pink champagne.
Instead I am clumps of gold soaking in whisky.
And I could drink my share –
a bottle in one hand, cigarette in the other.
Who needs a gun? My tongue's
sharper than Christ's cat o' nine tails.
Maybe that's why they say my voice is corncrake.

Though I'm no goddamn bird. Hey,
I intimidated Mr. Fonda himself.
But not my Spence, my Mister Tracy,
his eyes obsidian pools of light behind
glasses only he could wear.
He was my good-value-baked-potato
six days a week.

Sundays were for mass with Mrs. Tracy and the kids.
He was my intimate stranger, never
said he loved me.

Some say I'm a temperamental woman.
Feisty – even Spence called me a snake.
I can have my cake and eat it too.

Was it his drinking or his heart?
I'll never know.
I didn't see the funeral.
But Mrs. Tracy went.

I miss my Mister Tracy,
but I never yearn for death,
thriving instead,
a delicious flame burning between my legs.

And I plan on living for a long time,
at least until Miss Walter's funeral –
that's when I'll wear a skirt.

the

historical

Return Of The Men, by Renée Sheridan

Return Of The Men

They are men bent
on death, and life
with dents.
In armor –
some on two feet
or one. Praised
like the long ago man who
rode into a village
on a poor man's ass.
No palm leaves here,
but flags.
Red. White. Blue.
They limp along the road,
their cracked and filthy feet
kissing the lukewarm street.

Fingers, by Sue Messerly

Fingers

Right out of the Old Testament
malas in hands,
black-and-white kefayahs
like print on paper,
like the ballots,
their fingers marked.

Misbahas in hand,
hijabs shining black and golden beneath the sun.

A civic duty led by the god
who gave Hagar and Ishmael
the water of life –
and marked the Jews with blood
on wooden doors.

Marked purple ink
on their fingers
raised,
as a hijab is raised
when a woman is free.

Men. Women.
Faces the shade of Ishmael's sand
eyes blue as the Jordan River,
daring anyone to say
put your fingers down.

Sitting Bull, by Sue Messerly

Catching The Buffalo

Jumping Bull and Her-Holy-Door
saw the stars in the sky,
a message from The Great Spirit:

a black bull with red eyes,
anticipating,
like her Her-Holy-Door,
the birth of a son,
nine months later,
near the Grand River.

Ordained Slon-He,
accompanied by the
black bull with red eyes
who sits on the red ground,
when the sun rises and sets.

The black bull breathed into him
a victory over the Crow.
At 14 no longer Jumping Bull's son,
but a warrior:
Thanhanka Iyothanka,

a holy uttering only
the red-eyed buffalo,
and the Great Spirit could know.

He knows the buffalo's eyes.
His pupils as large
as it is young.

The young should run, the old die,
unified with the red dirt.

Thanhanka Iyothanka
communes with buffalo,
caressing its mighty thunder heart,
the two of them roaming
the red palm of earth
as Adam and Eve once roamed,
following the Great Spirit's footsteps

to a garden. But then
a warrior again
in what the white man called
Marmarth, North Dakota –

a small fish swimming,
a small hole,
a bullet through his back.

And Great Spirit wrestled him
as Yahweh wrestled Jacob
out of the garden
in the white man's Black Hills.

Now in the white mans'
Wood Mountain, Saskatchewan,
a spirit pure as rocks, he holds
buffalo at their necks
touching his eyes to theirs,
caressing the vibrating muscle
measuring the moment of return
to the red mud.

He shapes the mud black night
and sees a vision –
white men –
aflame
from Wood Mountain
to Little Big Horse,
the home of the sacred.

Thathanka Iyothanka
grasps the black red-eyed buffalo,
his pupils as small as he is old,
eating the clean meat,
reunited in mud,
wandering the sky,
the new garden,

and passing his armor to
Crow Foot,
his only son,

who catches the buffalo.

Lady Diana, by Sue Messerly

Lady Diana

You lived like a blade
of grass.
Jewels were your sun,
your water sweet
as Eve's navel
oranges, nourished
on Mother Nature's green.

With mother
you were fatherless.
With father
you were motherless.
With both
you were an orphan

going to St. Paul's Cathedral.
Just so they'd see you.
Just so *he'd* see you.

And he did.
Falling down the stairs,
vomiting in the toilet,
praying so loud
your throat went dry,
your tongue salty-parched

as the fortune teller's hands,
massaging your blue palms,
your jewel-burdened
fingers. Which was worse?

Abandoning God?
The conservative wolves at home?
The black land mines of your eyes
exploding in red, white, and blue?

They must have seen
your reflection in the dark
Mercedes-Benz,
heard your groans.
The camera lens zoomed.
The lights flashed white.

And men in white
massaged your heart
so your blood would flow –
but it froze, lay still
in the Paris dark.

I knew instantly that he would have a profound, perhaps disturbing, influence on my life . . . I realized that here was a man who did not want to marry. I . . . envisaged heartbreak, but just as swiftly determined that heartbreak would be worth the pain.

—Jacqueline Lee Bouvier Kennedy
The Eloquent Jacqueline Kennedy Onassis:
A Portrait In Her Own Words

Wedding Of The Century, by Renée Sheridan

Chorographer:
Jacqueline Lee Bouvier Kennedy Onassis
The Wedding of the Century

When she met him
she forgot him
for seven months –
until they met again
at Charlie and Martha Bartlett's party
in Georgetown.

He, voted most popular bachelor,
more popular than Rock Hudson,
invited her to Hyannis Point
where she met his family.

Patricia said her voice was the Irish wind.
Constipated. Eunice said
she was a rotten apple in the Kennedy Orchard.
Both said she had the face of a fish.

She wrung her hands,
ended up sitting alone,
watching them play flag football,

until the patriarch sat beside her and drooled,
you are so beautiful,
and she grew the courage to shout,
Toothy girls! And then

a courtship of
Byron, painting, conversing
about Churchill on long walks
on the shores of Cape Cod, Palm Beach.

He was poetically mad,
attractively bad,
and climbing.

No proposal
until she spoke to him
in French at Eisenhower's Inaugural Ball,
and he asked her

to translate ten French books
on Southeast Asian politics
for him. And she did.
To make him marry me,
she said.

He's going to be president.
The patriarch promised her a million
to love him. Truly.
As much as she loved her father,
drunk in New York City.

Stepfather Hughie gave her away
in ivory silk taffeta,
with a portrait neckline
she wore to please her mother.

Her muddy brown eyes
spaced wide on a face
shrouded in Grandmother's veil
of rose-point lace.

She lifted her face,
a sacrifice,
a ritual death of maiden-hood.

She kissed his lips,
consumed his body,
drank his blood, then laughed,
flirted with the groomsmen
inside the house of God,
mourned love lost –

a virgin chained to a chaste bargain,
a technicality.
It hurt. Was quick.

Then ended.

The White House Years, by Renée Sheridan

Chorographer:
Jacqueline Lee Bouvier Kennedy Onassis
The White House Years

Not love, but poetry,
the act of reading
Edna St. Vincent Millay—just enough

to make a baby, little people, expected
to play like Mozart,
speak French like de Gaulle
think like Churchill,
write like Shakespeare.

She only touched them
when their diapers were clean.

While Nanny Maud fed them
she hunted at Glen Ora.
While Nanny Maud bathed them
she rode Bit of Irish at Hammersmith Farm.
While Nanny Maud rocked them to sleep
she went to White House black tie dinners.
While Nanny Maud watched
Caroline play with baby doll Mary,
and John play with guns and swords,

she stayed in The Queen Room bed
reading Robert Lowell,
Kazantzakis' Report to Greco,
and Tennyson's *Ulysses*.

And then the lies
to reporters on her French
aristocracy, in bed, depressed,
making to-do-lists while her husband

did other things.

Pink Blossoms, by Renée Sheridan

Chorographer:
Jacqueline Lee Bouvier Kennedy Onassis
Pink Blossoms

She didn't want to go to Texas.
Those cowboys act as if they can ride.
Instead,

she flipped open
her red leather appointment book
and wrote *T-E-X-A-S* across
November 21, 22, and 23.

On Air Force One
he made Bloody Marys,
and they touched their glasses,
just like the first time.

And, for the first time in ten years
she was happy
in a pink Chanel Suit
with the pink pillbox hat
Jack loved.
*You're going to show these Texans
what good taste really is.*

Lincoln SS 100 X
side-by-side in the rear seats,
red roses between them,
in dark sunglasses
her white-kid-gloved hands
waving, like baby doves fluttering.

Take off the glasses, Jackie.
His last words to her.
Soaked by his brains, blood,
pieces of his flesh-colored skull,

the long stemmed roses
between them.

She tried to piece his head back
together
like a jig
saw
puzzle
and
held it together.
But his blood and brains
were cake batter
baking in her white-glove hands

Lady Bird said the car
was a bundle of pink blooming drifts
of blossoms.

At Parkland Hospital
she saw his body
in undershorts,
white from the loss of blood.
She kissed his feet,
his lips, his cheeks.
Father Hofer gave the last rights,
and she knelt in the corner,
said prayers for the dead.

Everyone insisted she change.
No. Let them see what they've done.
She wore pink and blood for hours.

On the way to the White House
Admiral Buckley handed her two dying roses,
retrieved from a trash can –
all that was left of her welcome
bouquet. She laid them to rest
in her pocket.

She would tell the children,
but Nanny Maud did
instead.

She went to the nursery,
her girl, boy standing tall.
Dressed in pajamas.
The thing to remember most of all, your father
was President of the United States.

Caroline wrote a letter to Daddy,
then placed her hand on John's
and wrote another –

to place in the 500-year-old
African mahogany coffin
where his face waited like a wax mask
from Madame Tussauds.

Birthing of Camelot, by Sue Messerly

Chorographer:
Jacqueline Lee Bouvier Kennedy Onassis
Birthing Camelot

Mother between her fatherless children,
on the steps of the White House North Portico,

they walk
to the place where he lay
as Lincoln had lain.

We're going to say good-bye
to Daddy. She is close
to the closed coffin covered
by the United States flag.

Dressed in black,
her pale face a shadow
behind sheer black lace.

She kneels and kisses the flag
covering the coffin.
Then Caroline kisses the flag.
And John does
as his big sister does.
Orphaned children dressed in blue.

She lifts the veil to Cardinal Cushing,
draws a cross upon her chest.
When will this agony end?
Accepts the flesh, the blood.

Caroline grasps her hand,
I'll take care of you, Mummy.
And John salutes his father.

Despite the Eternal Flame
her face is a shadow
beneath the black clouds,
the cold pouring rain,
God's angry thunder,
Satan's wind

blowing them to St. Matthew's,
and John's question
Where's my Daddy?

Finally, in Arlington,
embracing the flag that covered him,
the end of the service . . .
was like the fall of a curtain,
or the snapping of strings . . .

Jackie's widow weeds
the only thing
blooming.

Nobody could understand why I married Ari. But I just couldn't live anymore as the Kennedy widow. It was a release, freedom from the oppressive obsession the world had with me.

—Jacqueline Lee Bouvier Kennedy Onassis
The Eloquent Jacqueline Kennedy Onassis:
A Portrait In Her Own Words

Lucky, by Renée Sheridan

Chorographer:
Jacqueline Lee Bouvier Kennedy Onassis
Lucky

The weather was chilly and wet,
a sign of luck at a Greek wedding.

When she met the shipping tycoon
she was First Lady,
onboard the Christina
to meet the President's hero,
Winston Churchill.

In a simple, above-the-knee,
white a-line dress,
she captured the billionaire's eye,
her voice a seductive coo.

There's something damned willful . . .
There's something provocative . . .
She's got a carnal soul.

He invited Lee and her to
the turquoise waters of Greece –
not as a suitor, but
as her sister's fiancé,
relishing in having
the President's Wife
onboard.

For the first time she felt free,
childish, giggling.

But America became her enemy,
her children its prey.
No longer First Lady, but a black
widow through years of nervous breakdowns.
Depressions.
Pills.
Psychiatrists.

She found safety in the fairy tale
Prince within the Greek beast,
on his Island, Skorpios –
each of them forbidden
from the other
like Samson and Delilah,
his money – his hair.

They married
with a $2 million trust
he gave her in exchange
for the Kennedy money she'd lose

in his tiny Greek Orthodox Temple,
Panayitsa, on Skorpios,
attended by U.S. military men
he wanted to impress.

She wore ivory wedding lace,
white ribbons in her hair,
and wide-eyes behind the veil.

She kissed her billionaire priest,
her left hand weighted
by the 40 carat ring
he slipped on her finger.

No one can ever really know what goes on inside another person's marriage. However, one thing that can be said about Jackie's second marriage is that Aristotle Onassis gave her the equivalent of a royal dowry in jewels.

–Ellen Steiber
The Jewels of Jacqueline Kennedy Onassis

His Penelope, by Renée Sheridan

Chorographer:
Jacqueline Lee Bouvier Kennedy Onassis
His Penelope

A marriage of walking,
reading Socrates and
Out of Africa, swimming
in the Aegean Sea.

He leaves her notes, inviting her
to dinners on Christina
of pink champagne,
Greek and French food,
chocolate cake.

They tango on the dance floor
above the swimming pool.
My faithful Penelope.
He buys her an apartment in Paris,
gives her The Pink House on a hill,
sails to Corfu to shop for furniture.

Then, a red jeep, fur coat,
diamond bracelets wrapped
in her breakfast napkins.
For her birthday, a gold belt
with a lion's head clasp, her sign: Leo.

His faithful Penelope is always late,
smokes L&Ms, shops for Greek art,
spends a million each year on clothes,

and insists on a separate life in New York,
which a true Greek wife shouldn't do –

initiates conversation with her husband's guests,
which a true Greek wife shouldn't do.
Yiannis, do you think Socrates really existed
or was he Plato's invention representing
the Athenian philosophers?

Don't you ever stop to think?
Have you ever noticed the statue
in the center of Athens . . . a statue of Socrates?

She cries, mutters in French,
runs off into the misty rain.

I'm sorry comes with a gold bracelet
from the jeweler, Zolotas –

but the jewelry won't sparkle,
and there's nothing left
to decorate in The Pink House,
no more books to read.

Then, the $500,000 moon earrings,
designed by Ilias Lalou
to celebrate Apollo's moon landing.

Still, she indulged,
spending all she could, then reselling
the merchandise for a higher price.

She had money.
Liked money.
Loved money.

Aristotle Onassis rescued me at a time when my life was engulfed in shadows. He meant a lot to me. He brought me into a world where one could find both happiness and love. We lived through many beautiful experiences together which cannot be forgotten, and for which I will be eternally grateful.

– Jacqueline Lee Bouvier Kennedy Onassis
The Eloquent Jacquleine Kennedy Onassis:
A Portrait In Her Own Words

Tera, by Renée Sheridan

Chorographer:
Jacqueline Lee Bouvier Kennedy Onassis
Tera

She comes, dressed in black,
her big, bold sunglasses
a mask to hide dry eyes.

As the casket lowers
next to Alexander's
in the Panayitsa's vault,
in the tiny church they married in,

the women weep –
as Greek women do.
Not her.

Already thinking of lawyers.
Money.

She tries to frown, to look
like the widow she once was,

but her lips are an unhidden smile,
a smirk.

She lifts her sunglasses
revealing her eyes to the Greek
Orthodox Priest
for blood, flesh.

No longer the Greek widow,
the faithful Penelope,
now full-faced and marked
by money.

The Division of Camelot, by Renée Sheridan

The Parting of Camelot

Don't let it be forgot
that once there was a spot
known as Camelot. . . .

1.
Camelot was born back then
and you, John-John,
swimming in the womb.

Each time you kicked she spoke
in French. And then,
patrolling the White House

garden plots, hide-and-seek
with Daddy in The Oval Office,
and important meetings

of great minds, including you,
stroking Mommy's pearls.
When you sneezed while riding

near the orchards on Hammersmith Farm,
she never let you near the pears again.
It wasn't the pears. It was the horse.

John-John, no!
Daddy tried to be stern
as the First Lady.

Caroline, you, running,
never see you touched by
Mommy, who prefers the horses
on Hammersmith Farm

while Maud looks after
you and Caroline
that cold day. At three, you only
knew the color blue.
Photos, memories, real or only

photos the whole world sees.
And you roaming New York
on your bike, your skates, chased

by all the president's men,
the figures of your father.
Your bad boy cousins share

your name, blood, DNA,
yearning for seclusion
without paparazzi.

2.
There is safety in darkness,
a kayak floating on the Hudson's womb.
The stars the only safe lights.

Never when the sun shines
on ADHD, dyslexia,
tutors. Mother

pushing you to law school,
politics. Ignoring your need
for Shakespeare's dramas.

Never theatre, acting
like Marilyn. Filth.
She gives in,

hires someone to clean for you,
for the sureness of white walls,
the scent of flowers.

Even after she's dead,
you hide the *George Magazine.*

3.
Always parked at LaGuardia
where you ran with Caroline,
there is the only woman

hesitant to marry America's Son
in Cumberland Island.
The statuesque blonde

Mrs. Kennedy to-be. A role to play,
in Carolina Herrera dresses,
Botox, Lubriderm.

A temper matching yours –
until she sees your ankle
wrapped in white.

These days flying in a
Piper Jet Sota 252
in Manhattan, a stretch of sky

to Hyannis Port, for a meal with the Mrs.,
and the stars calling out.
But, soft! What light through yonder window breaks?
It is the east, and Juliet is the sun.
Arise, fair sun, and kill the envious moon,
Who is already sick and pale with grief.

The small star calls
your name, known only to God
the Father, the Son, the Holy Ghost
of Mother's past.
Mother of Jesus.
And you.

The blues of Hyannis Port and
the blues of the sky
divide like the Red Sea.

You are the new star
come home to a place
higher than clouds.

It is from numberless diverse acts of courage and belief that human history is shaped. Each time a [person] stands up for an ideal, or acts to improve the lot of others, or strikes out against injustice, he sends forth a tiny ripple of hope.

— Robert F. Kennedy

Moses, by Renée Sheridan

Like Moses

But no stone tablets.
Shakespeare in one hand,
a rosary in the other.

Like Moses,
he fed people.
Not only Israel's twelve,
but every color,
from every place.

He was the third
trinity of his family
his father, God the Father
his brother, God the Son,
he, God the Holy Ghost,
the only holy one

like Moses.
He climbed
still afraid of heights.

When he descended,
the Father and Son were
laughing with the mafia
and kissing women who weren't their wives.
He rent his clothes

like Moses did,
and never befriended
the underbelly of America.

Sam didn't like what he did,
neither did Hoffa, or the Father, or the Son.

Like Moses, he was
the only one holy enough
to see the bush
burning.

George Patton, by Renée Sheridan

I Am

David after Goliath,
William the Conqueror,
General Grant,

no ordinary god in this goddamn war.
My helmet shows the scars.
Ivory pistol, Cuban cigar
too big for Moses'
so-called burning bush.

The giant went down
with three small stones.
The stallion took one
on my way to Messina,
while reading iambic pentameter.
50,000 of my own bastards want to kill me.
Lucifers – they want to be god.
I am.

I tell the Bishop of Sicily
with the big black Bible
asking me if I read the book,
Every goddamn day.
I know
what he's thinking.
How can I be holy?
Ike says I don't know
to keep my mouth shut.

A nun lectured me,
said my onion eyes were open
in prayer, and for not kneeling
on the kneeling bench.
There were a few things
I could have said –
but, I am

a gentleman,
saluting with my cane.
But once the hat comes off,
they are all yellow bastards.
I don't kneel to passive saints,
or some goddamn scholar
who can't shoot.
I'll kneel at a man's bed,
place my purple beating heart
beside his head,
whisper something holy in his ear.
The best, that's what
I am.

"It is my opinion that the use of this barbarous weapon at Hiroshima and Nagasaki was of no material assistance in our war against Japan. The Japanese were already defeated and ready to surrender because of the effective sea blockade and the successful bombing with conventional weapons.

–Admiral William D. Leahy
I Was There

Enola Gay, by Renée Sheridan

Enola Gay's Baby

No one knew who hit her
with the bottle of wine.
All they saw was waterfalls
of wine foaming
like dark lipstick
blood on Enola Gay's blouse.

It took three years,
$2 billion for Roosevelt and Oppenheimer
to get her pregnant.

On April 12, 1945,
a perfect pagan day,
the kind of day God might
make for Adam, evil
in a garden.

Her offspring cracked the earth
ten time stronger than Helios,
blinding Hades.

They fell from the empty sky,
mushrooms melting the sexes
of Adam into Eve.

Enola Gay breast fed on fire,
feeding darkness –
the comfort of light
dismissed. There is no mother here

to turn the small light on
for a crying baby.
Ashes to ashes and dust to dust
70 percent gone in 42 seconds
or less.

...the genius of Einstein leads to Hiroshima.

–Pablo Picasso

the

literary

Words Become Flesh, by Renée Sheridan

Words Become Flesh

Miklós Radnóti was tried for "effrontery to public modesty and incitement to rebellion" due to his second book of poetry. In November of 1944, he was shot by Hungarian officers. In 1946, his body was exhumed. His widow searched his pockets to find a notebook of poems.

Miklós looks for poetry in rainbows
while working on the railway.

Miklós looks for poetry in water
while marching from Yugoslavia to Hungary
and sings when he tastes water from a bucket.

When they beat the old man to death
Miklós has nightmares – until
he seeps into poetry.
Some call it madness.
Miklós called it survival.

Miklós looks for poetry in black petals
covered in gunpowder dust.
His words in his pocket are his only burial.

His widow looks for poetry in his pockets
and finds the scent of black petals, now
vibrant red.

His killers don't recognize the aroma
or the taste of words become flesh.

They only taste vanity,
like Eve's apple in the garden.

Clay Boy's Pappy's Idea of Heaven, by Sue Messerly

Clay Boy's Pappy's Idea of Heaven

The wife's church has one idea of Heaven,
and I have mine –
all nine of my babies nice and snuggled in their beds.
Never seen anything prettier – that's Heaven.

Not that I don't appreciate the singing.
Sundays, after whisky and fishing at Snake River,
I smoke my pipe and swing in the hammock
to whatever song they're singing.
Sometimes I think the preacher man
has them sing extra loud, to make sure I hear,

says if I don't come to church Hell will be waiting.
I tell him, Hell is better than being with him up there.
He tells me to think of my babies.

He says be afraid of God. I'm not.
I'm a little like God's son.
We both cut trees and work with wood.
Except for the whisky, poker, and cussing –
but if God's son had a preacher like this one,
he'd do it too.

Well, I tell the preacher this, and he says
that I blasamey? Something blas?
And he says, it's like doing what Judas did.
His face gets all red and puffy.
He takes a deep breath and tells me
to read the good book.

And I tell him just because it's wrote down
don't make it so.

The Share Cropper, by Sue Messerly

The Share Cropper

Bent over, his shell of a back cracked,
he is the undernourished turtle,
his arms picking and picking.
His skin is as black
as the cotton is white.
His present and future
are a drop of water
in heavy air.

His brain is the weeds he pulls –
too wilted to think,
too dry to dream.

At night he cannot sleep
because of the bugs buzzing and hissing.

He is prairie grass with no space to burn.

Response To Lucille Clifton's Signs, by Sue Messerly

Response to Lucille Clifton's Signs

A world where birds walk
and people fly,
the sky is the ground,
the ground the sky,
the earth the sea,
the sea the earth.

Because we've ignored the signs
we drink dirt
and sleep in water,
until we are stripped,
straining for breath.

Tom Joad Speaks, by Sue Messerly

Tom Joad Speaks

I'm sick and tar'd of people describin' hell as fahr.
It's dust in your eyes, your hair, your mouth.
Ya' can't git 'nough water ta git it all out.
When hell's all ya' got ya' want hell –
that land may be a Bowl of Dust,
but it's got great Granpa's bones in it.
I'd walk a hundred mile 'fore I trade it for one orange tree.
That was 'fore I was free. Ain't it strange?
When ya' become free ya' lose ever'thing –
includin' your last sip of whisky.
Them rich men and their goddamn tractors –
ever' inch of dirt they cross kills me.
The fambly turns ta dreamin' and a run-down jalopy.
This han'bill says they needin' 800 pickers.
800 my ass – they print 5,000 and 4,999 start dreamin'.
Crawlin' like ants from Kansas, Colorado, Oklahoma, Texas.
Pickin' all day and ya' have ta buy your own sack.
God forbid we sneak a bite.
Those deputies have guns an' they'll shoot.

Mother Road is packed with Nashes, De Sotos, Model Ts —
a woman almos' bleed to death from the shootin'.
All of this fer bread and water –
ain't enough to feed a person.
It's easy for kids – give 'em peppermint and they're happy.
Candy's a lie – so ya' won't have to admit the truth.
Ma says we the good people, the ones makin' the world go round.
We're hungrier in green California than we were in hell.
I miss that dried red land o' cotton.
There ain't nothin' like home –
even if it ain't heaven.

Monologues of the Ladies of Steepletop, by Sue Messerly

Monologues of the Ladies of Steepletop

I will control myself, or go inside.
I will not flaw perfection with my grief.
Handsome, this day: no matter who has died.
                    —the last lines of Edna St. Vincent Millay

Steepletop, that place of naked wildflowers,
skinny spines with pink heads.
She said the steepletops would live
until the brutal winter came
to break their green necks.

Steepletop was dead and abandoned,
except for the steepletops growing
in the hills and meadows.
Eugen and I worked like Trojans-at-war on that place.

Steepletop had its own mahogany bar
right next to the sapphire pool
where we drank cold scotches,
and smoked Egyptian cigarettes.

Vincent held her scotch in her right hand
and looked at the painting
of a naked woman with two white birds,
one floating in the air, the other perched on her hand.

Now the narrow wooden staircase
becomes a poem,
each step a sound, a syllable, a word.

Her red hair never changed. Her face
was freckled one day, the next clear.
She had that much control.
But her words were wild
pen marks flashing across the page.

Here is this chair
next to the fireplace.
The fire looks glassy orange.
I turn on the small lamp next to me

and read Rolfe Humphries' translation of the Aeneid.
Now is the time to write. With a pencil.

She always wrote in pen.
If she wrote in pencil she'd need
Eugen's sharpener.
He'd been dead for one year, one month, twenty days.

I behead the pencil,
experiencing pleasure as the blade
slices parts of the head away,
to reveal delicious black blood
that bleeds on to the page –
each character calm, calculating.

She wasn't Catholic.
Pills were her beads to holiness.
One could never get too holy.

I am in total control.
My lines are very neat.
It is time. I lay the pencil down.
Now I am the baritone singer
living on Charlotte Street with my sisters,
where Kathleen will always be alive.
I must go upstairs to see them.

I don't know why she took so many.
Maybe a headache – hellish, lasting for months,
blinding her to everything but tiny black spots.
Sometimes her only relief
was to sit on the porch, swinging
into the black of winter.

I am dancing, the stairs are my stage.
The stairs are now my bed, and I am making love,
to all the men and women I've made love to before.

Now I am an actress as in lifetimes ago.
Ladies and gentlemen, here is my bedroom:
the first room on the right at the top of the stairs.
I have only two photographs – one of Norma and Kathleen
hugging each other, beckoning me to the space
in between.
Then there is Eugen, holding a flaming sword.

She hated the dark but she could walk in it.
She loved the fire blazing, but she relished the cold.
I remember she and Eugen floating in the icy Atlantic.

I'm burning – I need another cold scotch,
the Atlantic is right here with me
where it is blue-cold;
but all I see are narrow wooden steps.
Another cold scotch,
another rosary bead,
and the sea comes.
The turquoise waves blanket the steps
where the steepletops can live
away from the savage ice
that cracks them into fragments.

I dive, I dance, and finally I am
cold.

They said she broke her neck.
Oh, dear!
Oh, baby!
Oh, beautiful animal! Oh, sister!

Scarlett Dirt, by Sue Messerly

Scarlett Dirt

Peacock feathers in black hands,
Southern belles almost naked
in fluffy white warm beds,
the more cold, the more blankets.

Until the Georgia summers'
heat rays cut the heart of a lost Ashley.
Papa demanded you forget.

She listens, otherwise
Mrs. O'Hara will make her say
Hail Mary's all night long.

She and Mary looked alike,
but she was the beautiful one.

Sometimes her father talked about the land,
his favorite color.
Red.
When she was born he christened her
Scarlett.

When the sun burns her hands,
shines so bright, she goes to the back yard
where crows live in the stripped oak trees.
Her hands are small shovels digging
the cool wet earth –
the coldest part seeping beneath her fingernails.

She forgets that damn promise
and eats dirt.
That's where food comes from anyway.

The Horse, by Renée Sheridan

The Horse

Several young men, also flushed with drink,
seized anything they could come across –
whips, sticks, poles, and ran to the dying mare.
Mikolka stood on one side and began dealing
random blows with the crowbar.
—Fyodor Dostoyevsky
Crime And Punishment

I don't like much except reading,
hate feeding the horse,
scooping up shit.

I looked out the window,
saw Pop petting it, feeding it oats.

Pop said feed the horse first,
even in depression times,
he's the gas to get us around.
But he can't get around unless he's full.

There was a drought.
Most of the crop died.
Ran out of green stamps.
The grocer won't take credit.

Pop lost his job.
Mother gave birth to a loud baby,
split her milk between the baby and the horse.

We had the jalopy,
no money to give it gas.
Finally Pop sold it.
The new owner went to the gas station
for a can of gas,
said, *hell, I paid for the gas,*
least you could do is make it nice and shiny.

So Pop cleaned the jalopy up, nice and shiny,
and I snuck out the window, onto the roof,
and looked at that horse.
He backed away,
making that noise.

I remember *Crime and Punishment*
and the jewelry the man stole
from the nasty old woman.
Pop was both
jewel thief and nasty old woman,
two sewn into one.

I was going back to read
when I heard a big pop –
Pop's fist against Mamma's face –
or it could be the electricity was turned off again.
Couldn't tell which.

Mamma was crying.
I saw Pop get on the horse,
and knew he was going
to the BAR L – where just about anybody
gets liquor
for a price.

My room was dark.
Electric company turned off the power again
because Pop used the money on the horse.

I went downstairs for candles,
but there was none.

I couldn't see to read.
Then after a thought,
and then another thought,
and another one,
I told Mamma I was going to bed,
sneaked out the window again,
hid in the barn.

And waited for Pop to come home
drunk,
and talking to the horse,

giving it a love pat,
stumbling toward the house,
whistling some song.

I got down,
put the bridle on,
tightened the reins and
tied it to the back of the shiny jalopy.

It moved.
Pop ran on the porch with a flashlight
I should've thought of the flashlight –

could've been in bed reading about a horse
that died.

Actions are sometimes performed in a masterly and most cunning way, while the direction of the actions is deranged and dependent on various morbid impressions - it's like a dream.

–Fyodor Dostoevsky
Crime and Punishment

the

wolves

Liberty for wolves is death to the lambs.

–Isaiah Berlin
The Crooked Timber of Humanity:
Chapters in the History of Ideas

Even when we have driven the Jew out of Germany, he remains our world enemy.

–Adolph Hitler

Conversation With A Kangaroo, by Renée Sheridan

Conversation With A Kangaroo

I learned two things in prison.
Speak well. Never share power.
Even at night my head is held high
like the blonde kangaroo when he sleeps.

Wagner is god. His music is my religion.
I am convinced of my power. Intellect. Decision.

Dr. Morell says, *how can you sleep like that?*
Power.

The Landsberg guards knew.
Gave me the biggest cell,
overflowing with flowers and sweet pastries.
I had every magazine and book.
The head table was reserved for me.

Generals beg me to take the sleeping pills.
But God speaks to me
as I sip vegetable soup at the Berghof at 3 p.m.,
drink tea at the Eagle's Nest at 4 a.m.,
and when I speak with ice on my hands.

At Munich five thousand came to a beer hall
to hear me. One thousand were turned away.
Thousands more visit my office –
where there are pictures of Ford, Benito. Me.

The British honor an incompetent alcoholic,
the Americans – a cripple,
and the black parasites who killed Jesus.

Everyone knows nothing happens
except when I speak.

Soldier-god, by Renée Sheridan

Soldier-god

I was set up!

No! You fucked up.
If only you made it neat and clean,
instead of ground flesh
a sloppy joe bleeding over the bun.

I didn't fuck up.
I am marrow, bloody and running,
never to return again.

When you cut you only cut the bone.
Quick.
You took too long to kill.

I'm good at killing.
I'm good!
I won a bronze star.

Bronze star, my ass.
Gone.
The minute they found
the bastard's wife and children.
You don't kill women and children,
only your target!

They were my target.
Animals, newborn babes.
They all look the same to me.

Answer for what you've done!

I'm not a goddamn soldier.
I'm a doll made from the same paper
you'd draw knife sketches on
I can descend quicker than Jesus.
Loads quicker than that blink of the eye
the Bible keeps talking about.

Put that goddamn knife down!

I'm god.

Offering, by Renée Sheridan

Offering

If you kill a man by your own hand,
it isn't wrong.
There is a reference.

I'm invisible.
They come to me as if they can

see – these creatures
too afraid to show themselves,

seeing my hands, my knife.

But I don't eat them,
just things of the ground:
tree, bush, shrub.

I know
even before I know

that this is the fucker
who dares show himself.

It doesn't matter.

I kill
without them knowing
I'm in the same room.

Cannibal, by Renée Sheridan

Cannibal

I hunt, as a wolf hunts a chicken,
biting,
barring her from the sacred things
of God.
When my body slams into hers,
black shadows invade the corners
of her rooms. Demon lover,
my eyes shine, and my lips open
to a red canal, a poisonous tongue.
I explode
with disdain.

Jadeite Jim, by Renée Sheridan

Jadeite Jim

They say I'm a sexual deviant
to their virgins –
daughters, wives, sisters.
Biblically speaking.

Their sons, fathers, brothers –
I'm the only love they know.

Those capitalists can kiss my ass.
Judas' sisters and brothers –
I would kiss them.

Where are you, my son?
Sit on my lap.
Do to me what Ham did to Noah.
Don't cry.
This is how love
feels.

I'd give thirty pieces
to convert Judas' sisters to socialism.
I'd convert them for some other things.
I'll let you figure that one out on your own.

Mad Giggler Gone Sane, by Renée Sheridan

Mad Giggler Gone Sane

I've always known
change comes through barrels of guns.
But I was sensitive, humane.

How you could be the daughter
of a closed-mouth woman, I'll never know.
You get your hole talking

just to make your ass look good.
And these two days
somebody could have run over the hill

and caused trouble,
because you told that we didn't keep our guns
loaded. I'm tired of being the only one who

understands. I planned
for your treason years ago.

I look at my faults analytically –
none! But, weapons I got

for stupid-piss-ant holes like you:
claws, compasses, guns, dynamite.

All you stupid piss-ants hear this:
get nervous!
All my eggs are in different baskets.

But not your filthy basket.
Sodomite. Harlot. Jezebel.
I ought to shove my prick up your ass.
Man hole, woman hole – all the same

Like that hole in the ground.
People gonna go down that hole,
freeze to death. Burn.

We lost one white one.
We got one black,
and one blue –
another still in that hole.

And now you,
with your mouth talking filthy hole.

Your ass is grass.

We can't go back; they won't leave us alone. They're now going back to tell more lies, which means more congressmen. And there's no way, no way we can survive.

–Jim Jones
November 18, 1978, In Guyana
Hearing The Voices of Jonestown

Black Baby, by Renée Sheridan

Black Baby

Black Baby,
no turning back.
Drink tonight —
for we are under attack.

All my black-headed babies:
come to me.
It's not from the desert or the animals.
The devil's spawn is here
to kill me for doing God's work.

Our black boy babies
flew away.

Jim Junior, Tupper Tim, and Stephen are gone
throwing balls into baskets!

You said winning the game
would put the government to shame.

The Johannesburg government said crops
at the hill bottoms would grow.
They didn't say how daily monsoons
would roll over the crops
in waves so strong.

Surrender to this God-man.
You're going to live in a better land.

Come to me, my children, my grandchildren.
This is the word of God:
> *Come to me, all who are weary and heavy
> laden, and I will give you rest.

Black Baby,
it's time to die.
I want you to walk with your head held high.

Marci?
I need it now, the syringe.

Black Baby,
it's time to die.
I want you to walk with your head held high . . .

I am God the Father, The Son, and The Holy Ghost
and you are my children and this is the word of God:
    **This cup is poured which is poured out for you
    is the covenant in my blood.

I want you to drink from the planted cup.
I want you to let this love fill you up.

My own people betrayed me.
They left with our enemy Congressman Ryan.
If I hated more, loved less,
we wouldn't have this trouble.

Love will make us grow.
Love will give us the chance
to walk down freedom's road.

They say love is something to fight for.
Martin Luther King, Jr. preached love.
John F. Kennedy preached love.
Look what love did.

When out of man's hearts,
all hate is gone,
love will right every wrong.

My children who left with those spies
are dead. God revealed the bodies
of Congressman Ryan, his news reporters, our Judases.
But you, my children, belong to me.

Black Baby,
as the years go by,
God will tell you why.

Drink!
Go to the other side,
to that land of milk and honey.
Oh, my children, there's no reason to cry.
Drink from my cup.

Please get in line
before we run out of time.
Drink from my cup.
Only good will come.

Black Baby,
I want you to stand in line tall and proud,
and wait your turn for the planted cup.

Hurry! Be free of those Russian spies,
raping our women and hurting our children.
This is a sweet sleep.

You'll have what your mommy and daddy
never had,
and live in a better land.

Oh, Mamma! Oh, Mamma!
I remember as a baby
she'd rock me and sing:

As you grew up,
as the years rolled by,
you were the apple
of your Mamma's eye.

The first time I felt guilt was when
a little dog died,
and I wanted to commit suicide.
But Mamma talked me out of it.

Rock a black baby
in the cross top,
where your cradle for three days shall rock.

I am your father,
sister,
brother,
husband,
everything!

Partake!

Black Baby,
drink from this planted cup,
that will forever runneth over.

I have a cup.
Just because you can't see
doesn't mean it's not here.

****

Oh, ye children of little faith.

*Matthew 11:28
**Luke 22:21

He is a sadistic sociopath who took pleasure from another human's pain and the control he had over his victims, to the point of death, and even after.

–Ann Rule
The Stranger Beside Me

. . . you feel the last bit of breath leaving their body. You're looking into their eyes. A person in that situation is god!

—Ted Bundy

Those, by Renée Sheridan

Those

Most people believe the story
he told Dr. Dobson.
It was the pornography.

And then the miracle –
accepting Jesus
the night before his execution. No problem

answering Dobson's questions,
unless it was about Those.
He forgets how many religious leaders
he's converted for –

might make a jury of twelve,
governor, president, district attorneys,
change their minds.

When Dobson asks about Those
he licks his lips,
closes his eyes, blinks, twitches.

He thought of god a little these years –
since Stephanie broke his heart.

Years of meeting Those:
hair brown, parted in the middle.

Of course, he was exceptional,
saw god's face every day,
talked to god and god talked back
through a mirror.

white as the snow in Colorado,
Utah, Washington, the white beaches
of Florida where he met Those
thirty-six apples, placed by Satan.

Cannibalism is evil,
especially beneath the light
of his white volkswagon,
or the moon. Those faces,
all of their breath, the beauty
of Those.

the

domestic

Domestic Murder, by Renée Sheridan

Domestic Murder

I come through the door
as a cold night comes.
Cutting.

My hand on the blade,
her heart in gaps,
chaffed lips kissing her damp mouth bloody.
Good night.

Cold,
the handle in my hand,
her soft soul cutting the velvet of night.

Tears, by Renée Sheridan

Tears

He did it mostly at night,
at home. Drunk.

Beat her face
with his fists.
When she cried,
he laughed,
ripped her skirt.

She said to go
to our room.
But he said, *watch*.

She tried not to cry,
tried to smile.
Wanted us to think
she enjoyed it.

He turned her over,
swung his belt,
beating her red, black, and blue.

He put his pants on,
fastened the belt.
And left.

We would hear her whimper then.
But not this time.

For the first time in my life
I wanted to hear her cry.

For Worse, by Renée Sheridan

For Worse

Now these screams,
this yank of hair.
She's tired of dreams.

Each punch, each kick
to the ribs demands
obedience. Laughter.
When she collapses to her knees,
he kicks her face, flat on her back,
rips her clothes.
What do you think of that?

Her eyes are shut,
pretends she is dead.
He grunts, stands,
grabs a shovel.

Cold snow and hot blood,
her last incantation.
Frozen.

Prey, by Renée Sheridan

Prey

When I lay in bed,
he permeates
the corners of my body,
blocks me
from everything.
But him.

Blood floods
my arms and legs.
Freezing.

His bloodshot eyes bleed on me.
His lips open to yellow bones,
embedded in thick red gruel,
his tongue stretching, sliding.

He rams in me,
surging with energy,
exploding with disdain.

After he finishes,
he walks out the door
into another corner.

The Coupling, by Renée Sheridan

The Coupling

Heart rolls and bratwurst stew,
the scent of home for your sisters and you.

From tomboy to barefoot angel in LA,
a high school queen to hostess for good pay.

He saw you at Daisy's that June afternoon.
Sultry, foggy, and he wanted you.

His hand against your face a secret,
until he locked you in the wine cellar,

where you read Forward's *Men Who Hate Women
and the Women Who Love Them*.

The cycle: bruises, handcuffs.
I'm so sorry, babe.

You held copies of Forward's *Obsessive Love*
in every room of the house.

And then the move to Malibu,
just you, Sydney, and Justin.

Spinach leaves and cheese rigatoni, chianti
with family, the last kisses in the parking lot,

your mother's gold rimmed glasses,
lost in the gutter at Mezzalunas.

Then Ben and Jerry's for cookie dough ice cream.
When a waitress finds the glasses

Ronald calls, *I'll bring them after
I get off work.*

He greets you at the door, the glasses
sealed in a white envelope.

***

Your white Akita wails in the juicy heat,
blood from your neck on his fur and paws.

He led the neighbor there.
Neck, like Diamond Head,

stuffed with black strawberries.
Breasts, cut. Oozing cherries.

You wore a high-collard black gown.
Your blonde hair loose to your chest.

A martyr now faceless,
a crater in the ground.

The night falls gentle upon the earth
But hard within the heart of a terror-filled child.
There is no peace this night
But a sentry-like awareness of
Every noise, every movement
Within the house.

–Pamela Prentiss-Harrison
"There is no Peace."

Lamb, by Renée Sheridan

The Lamb

Thomas hears them
in an upstairs room.
Wrestling, he thinks.

Then Father says *honor*
to Mommy.
The way to honor life
is to take it away.

Now he remembers
Father as a lion.
He didn't believe.
But Father ate mommy,

and growled.
And Thomas ran
to the woods beyond –
the branches tearing at his eyes,
bark gritty in his mouth,
the wings of deer flies
clinging.

He wore pajamas, they said
with sad blue lambs,
sweat rolling down his legs.
And blood.

He hid behind a bush
unspeaking,
wiped the blood and smelled it.
Mother's.
The way Father taught him the hunt.

And he ran. Called her.
Asleep, Father said.
Like he said when she swallowed
sixty-nine pills. And Thomas called 9-1-1.
The white people came.

Long ago she sang.
But not tonight.

Tonight there is gurgling,
a growl.
Then running,
and dogs yelping.

He hid with them in the straw
on the doghouse floor.

Then Father,
panting,
as if he carried heavy things.

There was a noise –
the kind of sound a lion makes
while eating prey.
Then the counting of sixty-nine pills,
white like moons,
in the palm of Father's hand.

The dogs stopped yelping.
Thomas stood
beneath the moon.
He didn't know
he was standing beneath the moon
until the light hit him,
and Father's hands –
crushing the sad blue lambs.

Mark was severely beaten and sustained serious abdominal injuries, defense wounds, brain swelling, bruising on the back of his hands, blisters on his chest, and burn marks (from what experts believe was a soldiering iron) on his thighs and ears. His liver was almost split in two. Mark succumbed to his injuries and died.

–Christal Rice Cooper
The Altus Times
April 6, 2003

Mark, by Renée Sheridan

Mark

I shop at Belles and Beaus
for a blue onesy
and white booties, then

drive to the grave marked
by dead grass and weeds,
and a flat stone epitaph,
Mark Gomez
1986-1987.

The police said
his clothes were red.

I lay the onesy beneath the stone,
and then the booties,
as if I were dressing a baby

just before he climbs on a beer-stained couch
to sit by Mommy's boyfriend,
to feel his whiskered face.

Maybe he sucked his thumb, giggled.
Marked for death.

Must every mother cradle guns
shimmering like a twinkling star,
pacing the park
where the vulnerable
crawl and play?
Where he hunts.

I am at home, watching the news.
After ten years his sentence is carried out.
Imagine the sound
of his body cells boiling.

I walk into my son's room,
marked by life, asleep,
his body swaying with each breath.
His clothes are laid out for tomorrow:
red onesie, toddler jeans.

Someday I'll say I knew
I'd hold him safe –
but even now
my arms are empty.

the

lambs

Massacre of the Sacred Circle, by Sue Messerly

Massacre of the Sacred Circle

When father returns with the buffalo
they sit on the ground for the feast,
recalling how Great Spirit and his lover, Light,
created the sacred soil,
the apples and paw paws, the pine trees
decorating the delicious green air
in misty jade gowns,
breathing, streaming,
incense into the sky,
touching the Great Spirit.

Native man touched his squaw
within the round tipi,
and they birthed children,
who removed their moccasins
and played in the red mud,
and wondered when the lightning bug
stars would shine
within the blueberry bushes.

Then pale men came with sharp hatchets,
chopping the pine trees,
tearing skin from the men's scalps,
cutting the women's breasts,
filling the flesh with tobacco juice,
placing them in saddlebags.

The tipi is now ashes,
the apples parched.
Dead babies root for milk.

Worms scrawl within the circle,
so sick, not even the strongest bark tea
can heal it now.

Bergen-Belsen, by Renée Sheridan

Bergen-Belsen

This place of corpses —
death that disregards names,
does not care what was,
remains.

Workmen's tables with leftover debris —
human pelvis ashtrays,
white-boned furniture,
torn skin for lamps.

The blonde quick sand swallows
their breath — no longer God's balloons —
now red mud
for the maggots to nudge
as bulldozers
cover the dead.

In what April will this place become
liberated?

Between Two Girls, by Renée Sheridan

Between Two Girls

Every morning
Vater spread honey
on a slice of white bread,
gave it to me,
love in his eyes.

Every morning Father sculpted
his hair, molded his beard,
the way God said to.
He let me touch it,
said, "It's a sign of holiness."

I went to school
with her.

I went to go to school
with her

until Vater got promoted,
moved us to a country home in Poland,
embraced by green velvet.
Outside the gate,
a dusty madness.

Father believed they wouldn't,
still they came —
cut his beard, his hair,
and took him away.

I miss my friends, teachers,
Berlin City Park, Leipzig Orchestra.
Vater said it's an adventure
to add to my diary,
the red and black one with the swastika
he gave me for Christmas.

Mother says, stay strong,
says what to do if they come:
don't complain, be invisible,
pray all the time, never out loud,
lest they shoot you.

Once I ventured out front,
past the gate into the brown wilderness.
I saw them, moving sticks.
I heard them, moving sticks,
the violin, the flute, the fiddle.

They came for us.
Mamma said the best ideas are thought in prison.
Wondering where Mamma is.

I used to love fireplaces.
But after smelling the smoke,
they make me sick.

Mamma said to listen carefully,
I'd hear Joseph in the well,
Joshua shouting at the wall,
Moses talking to the Bush.
I hear nothing.

I have Mutter, Vater,
butler, maid, housekeeper,
gardener, cook, escort,
and governess.
I am lonely.

Lonely. Never alone.
My cells boil in sickness,
sick people, sick bodies,
my veins bleed.
Rats lick my wounds.

Mutter said we'd go to Berlin
once a month, stay at Kempinski Gasthaus Bristol,
have dinner at Costiera Italiana,
and go to the Leipzig Orchestra.
I'm so happy.

I miss our house.

I saw her house.

My lips tremble,
not from cold, too numb
to feel.

Only been back a day,
already miss the city.
Today I took a walk,
where I could see the stick people.
I saw her.
Probably my imagination.

Wide awake on wooden bunks
I asked the lady how to stay warm.
She said, "You learn to live on the lip of insanity."
I don't know what she meant.

Mutter is worried about the war.
She told Vater she's afraid we'll lose.
"What will happen to us?"
"It is insane to think we will lose.
We must not live on the lip of insanity."

Mother said, "Never lose the wits about you."
She said, "Deep inside you will always have a song
to sing to yourself, your people, and our God."
I can't. My throat burns hives.

I don't remember the words anyway.

Thou shalt not be a victim, though shalt not be a perpetrator but above all, thou shalt not be a bystander.

—Professor Yehuda Bauer
Holocaust Historian

A15647, by Sue Messerly

A15647

Day One
When the train stopped
they were there, two men

at the barbed-wire fence,
partially covered with snow,
silver shimmering through.

One of them examined Brother's hands.
Too big, he said.
The other held mine.
Small enough.

They sent me to the bowl factory.
Brother went to the other side.

Day Two
Brother appeared at the fence,
rigid with snow,
and threw a ball of bread over the fence.
Catch it!
Trembling as it flew above
the wires, collecting bits
of snow, falling to the ground.
My only light that of the cold stars,
now in my hands, this ball of bread,
and snow.
Eat it! he said.
I don't need it anymore.

Day Three
He came to the fence,
ashes on his face.
He threw a piece of cabbage,
pink and purple, like a jewel
flying in a world of gray,
velvet in my hand.

Happy birthday, little sister.
This is the best I could give you.
I don't need it anymore.

Day Four
I have been eleven years old
for a day. I am at the fence,
so cold, so hungry
that I touch it with my tongue,
relishing in the taste of metal
waiting – the starlight
my only way to see.
He never comes.

Day Five
It seems we are ahead of schedule
on making the tiny ceramic bowls.
I am assigned to collect eggs,
at least five dozen
for the boses and their families.
I hear the loud noises,
above the chicken squawks.
I smell the stench throughout the camp.
They're doing laundry, my boss says.
I know it isn't laundry.

They don't need it anymore.

Day Three Thousand Sixy Five
When she is liberated

today
she speaks
out loud.

1 With the hand of ADONAI upon me, ADONAI carried me out by his Spirit and set me down in the middle of the valley, and it was full of bones. 2 He had me pass by all around them - there were so many bones lying in the valley, and they were so dry! 3 He asked me, "Human being, can these bones live?" I answered, "Adonai ELOHIM! Only you know that!" 4 Then he said to me, "Prophesy over these bones! Say to them, 'Dry bones! Hear what ADONAI has to say! 5 To these bones Adonai ELOHIM says, "I will make breath enter you, and you will live. 6 I will attach ligaments to you, make flesh grow on you, cover you with skin and put breath in you. You will live, and you will know that I am ADONAI."'" 7 So I prophesied as ordered; and while I was prophesying, there was a noise, a rattling sound; it was the bones coming together, each bone in its proper place. 8 As I watched, ligaments grew on them, flesh appeared and skin covered them; but there was no breath in them. 9 Next he said to me, "Prophesy to the breath! Prophesy, human being! Say to the breath that Adonai ELOHIM says, 'Come from the four winds, breath; and breathe on these slain, so that they can live.'" 10 So I prophesied as ordered, and the breath came into them, and they were alive! They stood up on their feet, a huge army! 11 Then he said to me, "Human being! These bones are the whole house of Isra'el; and they are saying, 'Our bones have dried up, our hope is gone, and we are completely cut off.' 12 Therefore prophesy; say to them that Adonai ELOHIM says, 'My people! I will open your graves and make you get up out of your graves, and I will bring you into the land of Isra'el. 13 Then you will know that I am ADONAI - when I have opened your graves and made you get up out of your graves, my people! 14 I will put my Spirit in you; and you will be alive. Then I will place you in your own land; and you will know that I, ADONAI, have spoken, and that I have done it,' says ADONAI

–Ezechiel 37: 1 -14
read during the
Night of Broken Glass ceremony

The Big Jew With The Mathematical Mind, by Renée Sheridan

The Big Jew With The Mathematical Mind

November 10, 1938 1:20 a.m.

100 percent German.
100 percent Jewish.
100 percent Rich.
100 percent Big.

Six feet, four inches tall, 225 pounds

in an Orvis Steinbock Tyrolean trench coat
purchased at Stein's Mens' Dress Shop
for ten German golden marks.

It was after midnight,
1:20 a.m. to be precise,

standing outside his bank
Jacquier and Securius,
valued at over five million German golden marks
in stocks,

just around the corner from Gerber's Grocery,
in the leafy Grünewald district,
on Number 5 Rosenstrasse,
near the Red Castle,
and the Neve Synagogue,

where he had just come from
with his employees,
to pray for deliverance
from the darkness he knew
was coming.

He had a lifetime warranty
on the windows of glass
from France Meyer & Company,
but never had to use it.
Until now.

His bank of glass,
mutilated –
like a piece of meat, bloody,

ground into shards of glass insects
crawling –

the reflections of their fires,
crawling.

His trench coat looked more like a
Nazi-supporting German,
than a wealthy Jew.

But he felt the six-pointed star,
embroidered into the lapel.

All ye vermin, come!
Come into the city block!

His four employees
jumped like grasshoppers
into the city block,
crushed together, holding each other's
breath.

Vermin in the trench coat!
Into the city block!

It took three men to overpower him.
He labeled them by height
Nazi 1, Nazi 2, Nazi 3.

They tied him like a dog for fighting
to a 12 x 12 cement block
weighing 59 pounds
made at the Heidelberg Cement Company
located at Number 40 Rosenstrasse.

He remained
straighter than a vertical line,
stiller than stone –
Twenty-five lashes for resisting.

Another one,
he couldn't tell how tall he was,
and looked into his eyes,
cut off in certain places,
like a diamond. Cut.
The glass crushed beneath his boots.

After four lashes,
he bled.
Stop! Please!

Stop? You want me to stop?
Well, we'll have to start over, won't we?

Eight more lashes.

Stop? You want me to stop?

Twelve.

Stop?

The Nazi with the cut off eyes
added two tablespoons salt,
two tablespoons pepper
to his back,
like a rack of sacrificed lamb.

He was dragged away
by Nazi 1 and 2.

Nazi 3 and the man with the cut off eyes
carried the concrete block.

Neither the sacrificed lamb nor the block
were ever seen again.

The ax forgets. The tree remembers.

—African Proverb

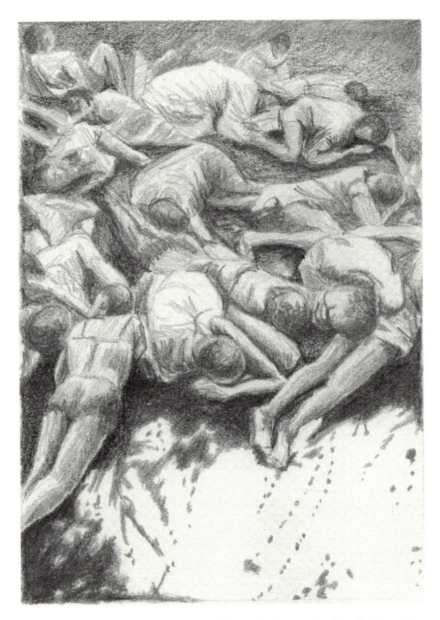

Falling Like Snow, by Renée Sheridan

Falling Like Snow

Each snowflake,
different from every other,
falls,
hits the ground
screaming,
then melts
and bleeds into the sewer.

Clear Water, by Renée Sheridan

Clear Water

Abidemi*
couldn't remember

his mother and aunts,
placing him in the
secret hole of the hut
beneath the table
covered with cardboard, blankets —
their cries, shrill,
the laughing ripping of clothes
from sixteen bodies:

old, young,
widowed, single,
pregnant, barren
ugly, beautiful.

Vaginas.
Nothing else mattered.

Abidemi's dirty fist in his mouth
choked his cries,

defining his mother's name:
Abuto**.

Their heavy footsteps changed —
silence no longer loud
and then,

the lamenting of blood, dripping,
saturating the blanket, cardboard,
his eyes closed.

This is how it is to be dead.

He stayed,
prayed to Banga***
to change the reality to
a nightmare, dreaming
in black and white,
his bones cold as pieces of white cloud
falling from the sky,
cold, thicker
than the lukewarm water
in the now dry pit,
watching for mother, aunts,
his tongue tasting the cold.

Banga had the power to change history.

His tongue moved into the taste of cold,
but it wasn't cold.
No pieces of cloud,
but blood, warm. Theirs.

If only bones, clouds could come to life.

Better stay. Pray
for the nightmare to come.

And he stayed.

*Born-While-Father-Is-Away
**I-Have-Hidden
***God-of-Clear-Water

Following his murder, Danny's family and friends established the Daniel Pearl Foundation to carry on his legacy, using music and words to address the root causes of the hatred that took his life. At Home in the World, published in June 2002, features 50 of Danny's best articles, illustrating his curiosity, humor, fairness, and his love of humanity.

www.danielpearl.org

The Head Chef, by Sue Messerly

The Head Chef

But then –
it's really no big deal,
been doing this for thousands of years –
slicing the head, neck from the shoulders –
like slicing a tomato, an apple,
or maybe an orange,
the juice staining our fingers like sin.

No one wore aprons, just masks.
Was it a sharp blade and one quick slice –
or was it dull – the kind you have to move
back and forth, cutting bits at a time?

Imagine a zesty knife on a lumpy potato,
hard celery, thick onion,
or a frozen cake filled with strawberries.
Or maybe the heavy neck of a deer,
bit by bit, blood rushing like the Red Sea.

It takes at least five minutes,
to slice the fat off raw chicken breasts.

I think it took nine minutes on the first dish –
and Daniel Pearl was American made.

All that mattered was the Head Chef,
whom he cried to.
Yahweh! Yahweh!
Why have You forsaken me?

The Resurrection, by Renée Sheridan

The Resurrection

The blood thickened and chilled her body.
His seed branded her tight white thighs,
stinging – more potent with each spill.
Oh, what a sexy guy! He makes her say it
over, over. Her blonde-bone body convulses
in the snow, and an owl calls from the bloody bed.
Run! She tries, leaves her corpse, dead stiff,
and stands in place where men are insects
to crush. She rips at his wings with her teeth,
and watches him crawl.

The Silver Penis, by Renée Sheridan

The Silver Penis

In the dark kitchen
I trace the invisible cuts
on my face, my neck,
my arms, chest.
My finger becomes the knife,
puncturing his handiwork on my wrists
until trickles form.
I breathe in the scent of blood,
as once I breathed him,
embedding the knife in my chest.
In. Out. In. Out. In,
till thick red ribbons of flesh
overflow the kitchen sink.
And my heart moves fast
inside of me
like he used to do.

I am a goddess seeking vengeance.
I laugh at the smell and sight,
thrusting into climax.

Two Miracles At Green River, by Renée Sheridan

Two Miracles At Green River

He never remembered their faces
once he dug the maggots from their vaginas.

They weren't real people
once he raped the corpses,
then dumped them in the Green River.

He never blinked
after arrest,
no remorse
after interrogation,
no tears
after the psychological evaluation,
never cringed
at the crime scene photos.

He made a plea deal
after they promised not to seek death.

He never felt guilty
after forty-five guilty pleas; but

he cried when Linda's father spoke:
. . . what God said to do is most difficult
when I look at you . . .
I forgive you and you are forgiven.

The court adjourned to two miracles.
A father's forgiveness.
A murderer's tears.

Nicole's Ballad, by Sue Messerly

Nicole's Altered Ballad

You met him at Daisy's
that June afternoon.
After a week of flirting,
he took you to Stellini's
in his vintage black Rolls Silver Cloud

and ripped your tight stretch jeans
for fast sex.

No longer Pinky's roommate,
but O.J.'s woman – kept
in a small Westwood apartment,

and a bigger apartment in Beverly Hills –
natural sunlight, and warm white
sofas, candles,

house in the deep canyon,
San Francisco condo and
cappuccinos at Ghirardelli Square.

Your parents thought the black Porsche 914
was for your 19th birthday –
never saw the black eye
behind the cover girl makeup
he was trying to make up for.

His divorce final,
you move to Rockingham
with white sofas and white candles,
flowers in vases, fruit in bowls,

Mamma laughed when he threw
the photographs lining the stairwell
down the stairs. Again. Again. Again.

You put them back up. Again. Again. Again.
Why do you bother to put them up?
Mamma said, *why don't you just keep them down?*

The Uzi he got for Christmas was kept
in the wine cellar.
O.J. said he would kill me if I left him.

9-1-1 brought lights, sirens,
your only defense, and then
his apologies, your pleas:

When are we getting married?
When will you quit screwing around?

This time the bitch had a name.
He pushed you
into the wine cellar, beat you,
locked you in, watched television.

No longer *sexy Nicole*, not even
O.J. Simpson's mistress,
but a girl afraid of the dark.

When he apologizes, you accept.
I'm pregnant.
I already have two, he says.
Demands abortion. Twice.

The morning promises
the biggest diamond ring,
and a quick push out of a moving car.

And finally, the quadruple-tiered,
white embroidered lace dress
with a straight skirt, mesh see-through portions
around the breasts, the long sleeves,
the short hair adorned with seed pearl ornament.
A necklace of diamonds. O.J.'s gift to you.

Then twelve long hours of dancing to Motown,
baby Sydney already in you.
Look at your arms. Look at your legs.
You look like a pig.

Until your piece of heaven was born,
and he called you *Nick* and *Sweets*
especially on the Louis XV bed.

Then, pregnant with Justin.
Fat ass!

Another mistress. Rough sex.
You refuse to take him in your mouth,
and he punches you in the forehead,
slaps you seven times seventy times.

$500,000 alimony, $10,000 a month child support,
and a 9-1-1 call. He knows your greatest fear.
To die by stabbing.

You make plans to move to Malibu,
while Sydney dances,
holding your gift of yellow roses.

Then, the family dinner at Mezzaluna's.
He wants to come.
You tell him no.

The kissing of knifes on forks,
spinach and cheese rigatoni,
Italian muddy-red chianti,
the whisper in Mamma's ear:
He'll always be my soul-mate.

You kiss Mamma, Papa, and sisters goodbye,
and walk the kids to Ben and Jerry's
for chocolate chip cookie dough ice cream,

then a bedtime story,
tucking them in,
a long soak in the tub,
candles lit –

not for a romantic rendezvous
but waiting
for Ronald to return
Mamma's gold-rimmed eyeglasses
sealed in a white envelope

Your white Akita's high-pitched barks
coagulate in the dripping heat,
wandering the foggy dark,
his bloody paw prints marking
upscale Bundy Street.

Placed in a coffin,
wearing a long-sleeved,
high-necked,
flowing
black dress,

hair loose
to your shoulders,
as it always had been.
Sexy angel asleep.

I can't stop seeing her face. Her face in the rain. Wounds on her body. She was so tiny. I try not to care, but if I do that, if I actually stop caring, then I stop being who I am. No job's worth that.

–Detective Tim Byliss
character from
"Homicide Life On The Street"

A detective sees death in all the various forms at least five times a week.

—Evan Hunter

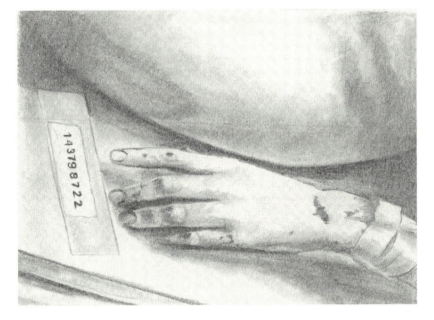

Savage Dog, by Renée Sheridan

Savage Dog

Every goddamn day:
murder, mourning.
It drains you. Me.
But that's why I'm
on this earth.

To hunt. Him.
A man like I am,
hunting him,
a man like him,
like a savage dog.

She fought him,
her hands curled
like Arby's curly fries,
her nails full of skin cells.
His.

When I first saw her, I knew
she didn't have any more blood.
He'd cut her all up
with a big butcher knife.

There's a huge difference
between a gun and a knife.
When it's a knife —
well that's personal.

At least he didn't rape her,
but then, we'd have his DNA.

And if I knew who he was
I'd go to his house, trailer, or whatever hole,
I'd say,
What do you say?
You mean son of a bitch?

God made a mistake
in letting you be born.

We finally figured out who she is.
Or was.
Deborah.
Might as well be another Jane Doe.
No dad, mom, brother, sister
cousins, uncles, aunts.

She doesn't have friends,
lovers.
She's about as missing as you can be.

At least that's what my wife says about me.
My kids don't say anything.
When I'm waking they're sleeping.
When I'm working they're playing.
When I come home they're sleeping.

It's up to my wife for them to know me.
It's up to me to know you,
you mean son of a bitch.

I will find you,
like a savage dog
kicking your savage dog ass.

We found your shirt you took off,
not to enjoy the pleasure of her breasts,
but to soak up the bright red blood
pouring from the holes
of her arms, neck, and chest.

She couldn't afford a hotel room,
her life consumed by a white powdery angel,
didn't have the luxury of the green forest
she tried to crawl into,
like an animal does when she is injured
and knows she's going to die.

Eight cuts on her throat alone.
No one deserves that,

except this savage dog,
this mean son of a bitch
I'm hunting
like a savage dog.

Beautiful Boy, by Renée Sheridan

Beautiful Boy

This is what righteousness sounds like,
the sound of his zipper's teeth, opening.

Even now I hear his groans.
You're my beautiful boy.

I hate that word.
My wife asks why I cringe, I say,
because of the beatings.

My empty food, my full vile,
cooking of my belly,
his pearl onion expelling over me,
in me.
God's mana.

He made me wait
till it dried, scraped it on a plate.
When I vomited it back up,
he put that on the plate too.

This is the Lord's Supper.
No room to move my tongue,
that weapon of bad burn,
fleshy pink elephant.

Even now.
I feel the stream of onions
scalding my tongue, throat.

I vomit hot air.
I feel beautiful.

I want to be frozen,
not his inebriated angel.
He was, is, will be.
I Am The Great I Am

his beautiful boy
shedding pink blood.

Pink, beautiful
marked out
of our dictionaries, books,
magazines, newspapers.

I scare my wife, but not
little boy blue, asleep,
swimming beautifully
in a pink sea of repetition.

The sins of the father.

I wake up with desire,
not for my wife.
For my boy.

Forgetting what I remember.
Remembering what I forget.

I put the gun, bullets
in the freezer,
in the garage.

My own land.
No man's land.

Women hold up half the sky.

–Chinese Adage

Katie, by Renée Sheridan

Miss Nobody

for every Chinese girl who reaches half the sky

Left by her mother
at a temple, abandoned, beside Buddha
in the dried weeds,
in the hot sun,
people passing by
the dark-olive baby
with blue-black hair,
then going
when they learn it is a girl.

The Chinese government demands
twenty nine thousand dollars,
must be crispier than lettuce,
in an archival white envelope,
no folds, creases, paperclips.
Nothing must contaminate the face
of Alexander Hamilton.

The government requires twenty gifts
from the adoptive parents
so they can have Katie. Twenty gifts.
The same amount given
to a newborn boy's parents.

If the gifts are not given
and the money not crisp,
she goes to the orphanage

where one woman
lives with seven babies
she cannot care for.
She's trying to forget
she cannot care
for herself.

Instead,
the plate of rice
she gets as payment.
Hours, days
in the pinewood chair.
Her back aches.

These babies,
two per bed,
no sheets or pillows
soften their sleep.

She leans toward their cries,
their dusty faces, and
wishes she were leaning toward a mirror
with hot pink lipstick on.

Outside,
she turns her face to the dark sky,
the rain drops spotting her face,
and will not hear their cries,
louder than any thunder.

Nothing is dearer to a father than a daughter . . . sons have spirits of higher pitch, but they are not given to fondness.

–Euripedes

Sick Joke, by Renée Sheridan

Sick Joke

We found your car
in front of Saks –
your favorite place to shop.

I went for Krispy Kreme and Starbucks
for the detectives,
told them you were okay.

I could've bought you a Manhattan penthouse,
but hard work
would help you understand the family business.

The apartment
was in a grandma and grandpa neighborhood,
with your own garage across the street,
and a pit bull named Sugar
who licked you like candy.

I left you messages:
when I held you
I believed
the genius of God,
always my baby.

And then the nightmares:
duct tape –
a wooden chair
tied to a cylindrical pole,
your black hair orange hellfire.

When Joshua, April, and their baby moved in,
just temporary,

I was glad,
until the new place is ready.
I knew you'd be safer then.

Joshua and I drove for hours
looking for your white Honda,
handing out posters of you smiling,
and twenty dollar bills torn in half –
bring information on my Kimmy,
and I'll give you the other half.

And there was your car in the driveway.

Kimmy, you home?

Maybe she went jogging.

The light blinking.
When I pushed the button:
when I held you
I believed
the genius of God,
always my baby.

New York State Supreme Court Justice Thomas Demakos sentenced Josh
Torres to 58 1/3 years in prison for the first degree murder of Kimberly
Antonakos. Torres will be eligible for parole on his eighty-first birthday.

I want to see him rot.

—father of Kimberly Antonakos
The New York Daily News